Lord of the Dance

Song by Sydney Carter   Illustrations by Jackie Morris

A LION BOOK

To Michael Carter S.C.
To Glenys Buckingham with love J.M.

Words and music of 'Lord of the Dance' copyright © 1963 Stainer & Bell Ltd
Foreword copyright © 1998 Sydney Carter
Story text copyright © 1998 Lion Publishing
Illustrations copyright © 1998 Jackie Morris
This edition copyright © 1998 Lion Publishing

The moral rights of the author and illustrator
have been asserted

Published by
Lion Publishing
4050 Lee Vance View, Colorado Springs, CO 80918, USA
ISBN 0 7459 3898 1

First UK edition 1998
First US edition 1999
10 9 8 7 6 5 4 3 2 1 0

Story text retold from the Bible

Library of Congress CIP data applied for

Typeset in 11.5/15 Baskerville MT Schoolbook
Printed and bound in Singapore

Foreword

*I*t was not until I joined a folk-club that I realized how, by dancing, you might express what you could not express in any other way.

It was in a folk-club, too, that I first heard of the Shakers. They were originally part of a religious movement called the Quakers who, instead of worshipping quietly, began to leap about, sing and argue. They got into trouble with their neighbours and the police and left England for America in 1774.

Singing and dancing became part of their worship. (They made wonderful furniture but that's another story!)

Here is part of one of the songs they sang and danced to:

'Tis the gift to be simple
'Tis the gift to be free
'Tis the gift to come down
Where we ought to be
And when we find ourselves
In the place that's right
It will be in the valley
Of love and delight…

I wrote my own song 'Lord of the Dance' to salute the Shakers. That was in 1963. Since then, many schools have written to me and sent photographs of their children dancing 'Lord of the Dance' and acting the parts of Mary and others who witnessed Jesus' resurrection. (These include, if I remember rightly, some frustrated devils!)

This song is a celebration of hope and encouragement and should be sung joyfully. Sometimes, for a change, I sing the whole song in the present tense—'I dance in the morning when the world is begun…'

It is worth a try!

Sydney Carter

Before the world was made, there was God.

God spoke, and the powerful Word called the whole world into being.

Angels danced in the heavens.

The sun shone upon the earth by day, and the moon and the stars lit up the night-time.

Sleek sea creatures swam in the deepest oceans.

Lightning flashed across the sky, and the clouds brought hail and snow as the mighty winds blew.

I danced in the morning
When the world was begun,

The hills and mountains rose above the waters. Tall trees grew and gave their shade, and fruit trees yielded a rich harvest.

Animals of every kind were made to live in this beautiful world. Scaly reptiles slithered among the rocks. Birds called to one another with their strange and lovely melodies.

Then people danced upon the earth.

And the whole world praised God.

John 1:1–5; Psalm 148

And I danced in the moon

And the stars and the sun,

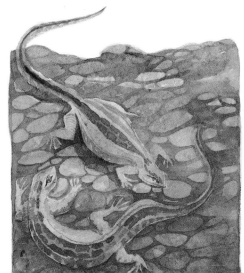

In the beginning, God made a world that was beautiful and good.

But the people God had made chose to live their lives as they thought best. One terrible mistake followed another. Soon their world was a harsh world, full of sadness and weeping.

Many, many years later, the one who had created the world came to this earth as a human being. He dwelt among people, to show them the way back to being friends with God.

This is how it happened: the angel Gabriel brought a message to a young woman named Mary, telling her that God wanted her to be the mother of a very special baby. She must name the baby Jesus, but he would be known as God's own son.

Mary must have loved God, for she agreed.

And I came down from heaven
And I danced on the earth,

At Bethlehem

I had my birth.

*M*onths went by, and the day when the baby would be born drew nearer. But an order came from the Roman emperor who ruled the land: everyone must travel to the place their family came from to put their names on a register. The emperor planned to make all his subjects pay taxes.

Mary had to travel to Bethlehem with Joseph, the man she planned to marry. There, far from her home, where the only place she could find to stay was a stable for the animals, Mary's baby was born.

Mary wrapped her baby in swaddling clothes and laid him in a manger.

John 1:14; Luke 1:26–38, 2:1–7

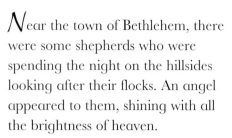

Near the town of Bethlehem, there were some shepherds who were spending the night on the hillsides looking after their flocks. An angel appeared to them, shining with all the brightness of heaven.

The shepherds were terrified.

As they cowered in fear, the angel spoke: 'Do not be afraid. I am here with good news for you—news that will bring joy to all the world. This very day, in Bethlehem, has been born the one God promised to send to rescue people from sorrow and darkness.

'Here is a sign, so that you will know that what I say is true. You will find the baby wrapped in swaddling clothes and lying in a manger.'

Suddenly a great company of angels appeared, praising God and singing, 'Glory to God in the highest, and on earth, peace.'

Dance, then, wherever you may be,

I am the Lord of the Dance, said he,

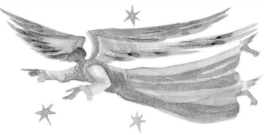

When the angels had gone,
the shepherds said to each other,
'Let us go to Bethlehem, to see if
this is really true.'

So they hurried off and they
found Mary and Joseph, and the
baby in the manger.

Then the shepherds returned to
their flocks. As they went, they
sang praises to God.

Luke 2:8–20

And I'll lead you all, wherever you may be,

And I'll lead you all in the Dance, said he.

When Jesus grew up, he began his very special work.

He spent his time travelling the land, telling people of God's love. Wherever he went, he showed that love in action: befriending the lonely, healing those who were sick, and telling people that they could lay aside all the wrongdoing that had spoiled their lives. They could live as God's friends, and even as God's children, calling God their Father.

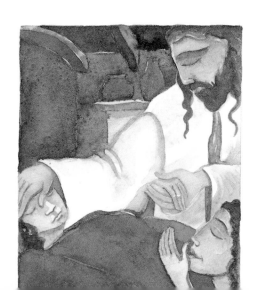

I danced for the scribe

And the pharisee,

But they would not dance
And they wouldn't follow me.

Among his own people were those who thought they knew all about God. Some were scribes; they had spent long years poring over the ancient writings of the Jews. They knew the stories of how God had always taken care of them. They knew the laws that God had given to lead people in the way of goodness. Many of these people also belonged to a group called the Pharisees. They were devoted to working out how God's law applied to every little thing that happened in life.

Sadly, their knowledge had made many of them proud. They were zealous to do what was right; but they had forgotten how to love, how to forgive.

And they hated Jesus and the things he said and did.

Luke 5:17–26

One day, Jesus was standing on the shore of the lake called Galilee. People pushed their way up to him to hear what he had to say about God.

Jesus noticed two fishing boats that had been pulled up onto the shore. One belonged to a man named Simon, and the other to his fellow workers, James and John.

Jesus got into Simon's boat and asked him to push it out into the water. From there he sat in the boat and taught the crowd.

I danced for the fishermen,

For James and John—

They came with me

And the Dance went on.

When Jesus had finished, he said to Simon, 'Push your boat out into deep water, and you and your fellow workers can let down your nets for a catch.'

'Master,' replied Simon, 'we fished all night and caught nothing. But if you wish, I will do as you ask.'

So he did. The nets became so full he had to call to the others to come quickly, for fear his boat would sink. Even together, they struggled to bring the catch to shore.

Simon looked at Jesus with fear and wonder. Falling on his knees he said, 'Go on your way. I'm not worthy to be with you.' The others did the same.

Jesus replied, 'Don't be afraid. From now on you will be gathering people as once you gathered fish.'

They pulled the boats onto the shore, left everything and followed Jesus.

Luke 5:1–11

One day, some people brought their little children to Jesus, for him to bless them. His closest followers, his disciples, saw them and scolded them. How dare they trouble Jesus with something so unimportant!

Dance, then, wherever you may be,
I am the Lord of the Dance, said he,

But Jesus called the children to him and said, 'Let the children come to me and do not stop them, because the Kingdom of God belongs to little ones like these.

'Indeed, whoever does not accept the Kingdom of God like a child will never enter it.'

Luke 18:15–17

And I'll lead you all, wherever you may be,
And I'll lead you all in the Dance, said he.

In the land where Jesus lived, one day in seven was special: it was a day of rest, and a day for the people to remember the God who had made the world. They would go to their meeting-place, the synagogue, and hear again the stories of their people and the laws that God had given. The people called this day the sabbath.

Now it was God's own laws that told them to rest on the sabbath, and the scribes and the Pharisees were anxious to keep this law as perfectly as they could. One sabbath day, Jesus went to the synagogue and spoke to the people there.

I danced on the Sabbath

And I cured the lame;

The holy people

Said it was a shame.

The scribes and Pharisees who had gathered there were watching closely. Everyone knew that Jesus could heal people, and there in the synagogue was a man whose arm was paralysed.

Jesus called the man to come to the front. Then he asked a question: 'I ask you, what does our law allow us to do on the sabbath? To help or to harm? To save a person's life or destroy it?'

He looked around at the people. Then he said to the man, 'Stretch out your arm.' As the man did so, it became strong again.

The scribes and Pharisees were filled with rage. They began to discuss among themselves what they could do to silence Jesus.

Luke 6:6–11

For three years Jesus went about his work of helping and healing, and many people loved him.

The scribes and the Pharisees hated him. They wanted to have him put to death, but they were afraid to do so, because he had so great a following. Perhaps they could have him put to death secretly?

Then came the chance they had been waiting for: at the time of a great festival known as Passover, Jesus and his followers came to the city of Jerusalem. One of Jesus' close friends told them where they could come and arrest him. One night, as he prayed to God in an olive grove named Gethsemane, soldiers came and hustled Jesus away.

They whipped and they stripped

And they hung me on high

And they left me there

On a cross to die.

They told lies about him. They made up a story that he planned to rebel against the Romans who ruled the land. The Roman governor did not really believe the story, but Jesus' enemies had done their work well. When the governor offered to set Jesus free, the crowd had turned against him. 'Crucify him, crucify him,' they shouted.

Roman soldiers took their orders. They whipped Jesus. They stripped him of his clothes. They led him to a hillside outside the city and laid him on a cross of wood. Then they drove great iron nails through his hands and feet and stood the cross upright in the ground.

Matthew 26—27:36

On the day that Jesus was crucified, two other men—both criminals—were led out to die. They were crucified, one on Jesus' right, one on Jesus' left.

Jesus said a prayer to God. 'Father, forgive them, they don't know what they are doing.'

The leaders of the people jeered at Jesus. 'He saved others. Let's see if he can save himself.'

The soldiers mocked him. 'You are charged with wanting to be the king of your own people. Save yourself if you're so great!'

One of the criminals hurled insults at him. 'Aren't you meant to be the one sent by God to save our people? If you are, then save yourself and us.'

Dance, then, wherever you may be,
I am the Lord of the Dance, said he,

And I'll lead you all, wherever you may be,
And I'll lead you all in the Dance, said he.

*B*ut the other man spoke sharply. 'Beware of God,' he warned. 'We are getting the due punishment for our crime. This man is getting the same punishment, yet he has done no wrong.'

He spoke to Jesus: 'Remember me when you come as King.'

And Jesus replied, 'I promise you that today you will be in paradise with me.'

Luke 23:32–43

It was about twelve o'clock on the day Jesus was crucified that the sun stopped shining. Darkness covered the whole country until three o'clock.

Jesus called out to God in a loud voice, 'Father! Into your hands I place my spirit!' He said this and died.

Now, among the powerful religious people who had plotted against Jesus were some who had not agreed with what had been done. One of these was a rich man named Joseph, who came from the town of Arimathea.

I danced on a Friday
When the sky turned black—
It's hard to dance
With the devil on your back.

They buried my body

And they thought I'd gone

But I am the Dance

And I still go on.

He asked for permission to take the body of Jesus. He took it down from the cross, wrapped it in a linen sheet and placed it in a tomb cut like a cave out of solid rock. A round stone door was rolled in place over the entrance.

There was no time to prepare the body properly for its burial, for now the sun was setting and the sabbath day of rest was beginning.

Joseph and the others who had come to the tomb with him went away, in deepest sorrow. It seemed that they would never sing and dance again.

Luke 23:44–56

John sat in the darkened room and wept.

He called to mind the tumultuous years he had spent as a follower of Jesus.

The day on the shore of Lake Galilee, when Jesus had told them where to fish for the biggest catch they had ever made… and then called them to give up their old way of life to follow him.

John had done just that. He had seen people healed: Jesus had made the lame walk, the blind see, the dead come back to life. He believed with all his heart that Jesus did this because he was from God.

He had heard the stories Jesus told—stories that painted a picture of God as kind and strong, caring for people as a good shepherd cares for his sheep.

He remembered the last meal he had shared with Jesus, when Jesus had told them to love one another.

Dance, then, wherever you may be,
I am the Lord of the Dance, said he,

And I'll lead you all, wherever you may be,

And I'll lead you all in the Dance, said he.

And then he remembered something puzzling that Jesus had said: 'In a little while you will not see me, and then a little while later you will see me…'

Then Jesus had said, 'I am telling you the truth: you will cry and weep, but the world will be glad; you will be sad, but your sadness will be turned into gladness.'

He had said it again: 'Now you are sad, but I will see you again, and your hearts will be filled with gladness, the kind of gladness that no one can take away from you.'

As he remembered, it seemed to John that the room was filled with angels. And for a few moments, he believed with all his heart that he would dance again.

John 16:19, 20, 22

Jesus was put to death on a
Friday. Then came the sabbath
day of rest.

Very early on Sunday morning,
the women who had gathered to
watch as Jesus was laid in the tomb
returned. They brought the spices
that were used in preparing a body
for burial.

They found the stone rolled
away from the entrance to the
tomb. Stooping a little, they went
inside.

To their astonishment, the tomb
was empty. The body simply was
not there.

Suddenly two people in bright
shining clothes stood by them. The
women bowed down to the ground
in fear, but then the people spoke:
'Why are you looking among the
dead for one who is alive? He is not
here; he has been raised to life.
Remember what he said: he told
you he would be crucified and then
would rise again.'

They cut me down
And I leapt up high;
I am the life
That'll never, never die;

I'll live in you

If you'll live in me —

I am the Lord

Of the Dance, said he.

The women remembered Jesus' words. But that was not all. As the day went by, people saw him with their own eyes.

For many days afterwards, Jesus appeared among groups of his astonished followers. He talked with them. He ate with them. He showed them the marks of the nails in his body… he was truly Jesus, yet somehow different—more alive than ever before.

After forty days, Jesus said goodbye. He told his friends not to worry: even though they would no longer see him, he would come close to them in a new and special way.

Then Jesus was taken up to heaven. As his closest followers watched, a cloud hid him from their sight.

Luke 24:1–8; Acts 1:3–9

John was remembering again. He was remembering the days when he had followed Jesus the length and breadth of their little country. He was remembering Jesus' kindness—to them, and to all those who came to see him: the sick, the aged, the little children, the rich, the poor, the humble, the proud… Jesus had loved them all.

Dance, then, wherever you may be,
I am the Lord of the Dance, said he,

And I'll lead you all, wherever you may be,

And I'll lead you all in the Dance, said he.

And he remembered Jesus' words: 'Whoever loves me will obey my teaching, and my Father and I will come to that person and live with them...

'I am telling you this while I am still with you. The helper is the Holy Spirit, whom the Father will send in my name. The Holy Spirit will teach you everything and make you remember all that I have told you.

'Peace is what I leave with you.'

And John knew that he and the others who followed Jesus must live to tell the amazing story of Jesus, and let God's love shine out in everything they did.

John 14:23, 25–27

Adapted from a Shaker melody by Sydney Carter

I danced in the mor-ning When the world was be-gun, And I danced in the moon And the stars __ and the sun, And I came down from hea-ven And I danced on the earth, At Beth-le-hem I had my birth. *Dance, then, where-e-ver you may be, I am the Lord of the Dance, said he, And I'll lead you all, where-e-ver you may be, And I'll lead you all in the Dance, said he.*

Lord of the Dance

I danced in the morning
When the world was begun,
And I danced in the moon
And the stars and the sun,
And I came down from heaven
And I danced on the earth,
At Bethlehem
I had my birth.
Dance, then, wherever you may be,
I am the Lord of the Dance, said he,
And I'll lead you all, wherever you may be,
And I'll lead you all in the Dance, said he.

I danced for the scribe
And the pharisee,
But they would not dance
And they wouldn't follow me.
I danced for the fishermen,
For James and John—
They came with me
And the Dance went on.
Chorus

I danced on the Sabbath
And I cured the lame;
The holy people
Said it was a shame.
They whipped and they stripped
And they hung me on high
And they left me there
On a cross to die.
Chorus

I danced on a Friday
When the sky turned black—
It's hard to dance
With the devil on your back.
They buried my body
And they thought I'd gone,
But I am the Dance
And I still go on.
Chorus

They cut me down
And I leapt up high;
I am the life
That'll never, never die;
I'll live in you
If you'll live in me—
I am the Lord
Of the Dance, said he.
Chorus

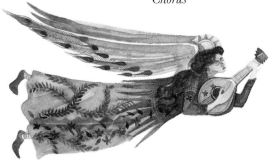

A simple dance to 'Lord of the Dance'

For the verse

Hold hands in a row of three. The rows of three stand one behind the other to make a big circle around the room and move in an anti-clockwise direction.

Step as follows on the first and third beats of each bar (so 'I *danced* in the *morn*ing when the *world* was be*gun*'):

1 Step forward on your left foot.
2 Step forward on your right foot.
3 Step forward on your left foot.
4 Rock back on your right foot.
Repeat for each line of the verse.

For the chorus

Make a right-hand star by joining right hands in the middle and skip round for the first two lines.

Make a left-hand star and skip round the other way for the last two lines.